Candle Making Like A Pro

A Complete Guide on How to Make Perfect Candles at Home for Fun & Profit

Vanessa D. Langton
Copyright© 2015 by Vanessa D. Langton

Candle Making Like A Pro

Copyright© 2015 Vanessa D. Langton

All Rights Reserved.
Warning: The unauthorized reproduction or distribution of this copyrighted work is illegal. No part of this book may be scanned, uploaded or distributed via internet or other means, electronic or print without the author's permission. Criminal copyright infringement without monetary gain is investigated by the FBI and is punishable by up to 5 years in federal prison and a fine of $250,000. (http://www.fbi.gov/ipr/).
Please purchase only authorized electronic or print editions and do not participate in or encourage the electronic piracy of copyrighted material.

Publisher: Living Plus Healthy Publishing

ISBN-13: 978-1507586068

ISBN-10: 150758606X

Disclaimer

The Publisher has strived to be as accurate and complete as possible in the creation of this book. While all attempts have been made to verify information provided in this publication, the Publisher assumes no responsibility for errors, omissions, or contrary interpretation of the subject matter herein. Any perceived slights of specific persons, peoples, or organizations are unintentional.

This book is not intended for use as a source of legal, business, accounting or financial advice. All readers are advised to seek services of competent professionals in the legal, business, accounting, and finance fields.

The information in this book is not intended or implied to be a substitute for professional medical advice, diagnosis or treatment. All content contained in this book is for general information purposes only. Always consult your healthcare provider before carrying on any health program.

Table of Contents

Introduction 5

Chapter 1: A Brief History of Candle Making 9

    Candles in History 14
    Candles Today 18

Chapter 2: Safety First 19

    Candle Making Safety Tips......................... 19
    Candle Burning Safety Tips........................ 22

Chapter 3: Candle Making Supplies 25

    Wax Melting Supplies 25
    Wick Supplies 26
    Candle Wax Supplies................................... 29
    Fragrance Supplies....................................... 31
    Colorant Supplies... 33
    Candle Molds and Containers.................... 35
    Miscellaneous Items..................................... 38

Chapter 4: The Basics 41

Beginning Candle Making 42

Throwing in the Scent 44

Putting in the Colorant 46

Readying the Wicks, Containers and Molds
.... 48

Pouring the Wax 49

Cooling Wax and Releasing Molds 49

Troubleshooting 50

Chapter 5: Making More Elaborate Candles . 57

Gel Candles 57

Soda Fountain Candles 60

Whipped Wax 61

Sand Candles 63

Layered Candles 67

Ice Candles 68

Balloon Candles 69

Beeswax Candles 70

Chapter 6: Candles as Gifts 73

Lace-Trimmed Candles as Gifts 73

Easter Candle Holder Gift Idea 74

Christmas Gift Ideas 76

Baby Shower Candle Gifts 77

Gift Wrapping Ideas 78

Chapter 7: Turning Your Candle Making into a Business 79

Research the Business 79

Find a Supplier 80

Don't Forget Your Time 81

Create a Marketing Plan............................. 82

What to Sell Your Product for? 83

Whom to Sell to 84

Keeping in Touch 86

Conclusion 87

Introduction

What is more romantic than a spa tub ringed with softly lit candles or candles on the fireplace, glowing brightly over your meal? Candles have long been associated with love and romance. They make beautiful gifts for just about anyone and, when scented, they offer you an aroma that brings out the best in people. When there's a storm and the lights go out, candles make for a peaceful environment as you wait out the storm.

Not long ago, candles were more utilitarian, used to light rooms at night in homes that had no electricity. Such candles were simple and usually unadorned. They were used for ceremonial purposes in religious ceremonies and, in many parts of the world, they still are used in that fashion. These candles are also unadorned in most cases. You, however, have a wealth of information available to you in this guide to help you make candles that are not only functional but beautiful.

Perhaps this is your first attempt at making candles or maybe you've made some candles and are considering starting a candle making business. This guide will, of necessity, start with the premise that you don't know anything about candle making and will show you how to make candles of increasing complexity so you can make just about any type of candle, including dipped candles or tapers, sand candles and pillar candles.

There are actually many different types of candles you'll be able to make after reading this guide. These include candles of many different shapes, sizes and candle making techniques. Let's look at the various types of candles you'll be able to make after reading this guide.

- **Container Candles.** This is a candle in which you pour the hot wax into a container that has a wick affixed to it. The container you pour the wax into can be anything and the candle forms the shape of the candle. The candle is burned in the container as well. Glass jars are often used because you can see the whole candle and the process offers you the chance to put in layers of candle wax.

- **Votive Candles.** These commonly used candles are a split between a pillar candle and a container candle. They are usually free standing candles in a cylindrical shape and are placed into a small glass container. As the candle burns down, it forms the shape of the glass container that it is placed in.

- **Pillar Candles.** These are molded candles that are thick enough to stand up on their own. They can burn freely on a heat-resistant surface or can be placed into a large container. They tend to burn evenly and not drip wax onto the surface they are placed on.

- **Dipped Candles.** Also called tapered candles, these are dipped multiple times by placing a primed wick into hot wax over and over again until a thin candle is formed with a wick at the top. Multiple layers of wax make up the candle.

- **Rolled Candles.** These are often made with pliable beeswax sheets that can be tightly rolled around a wick until it makes a candle that is much the shape of a tapered candle except it is not tapered at the top. These candles tend to be textured because the sheets used are textured as well.

- **Tea Light Candles.** These are tiny cylindrical candles that are housed within an aluminum holder and placed within a glass container. The height is less than an inch.

- **Hurricane Candles.** These are fun candles that have shells or dried flowers imbedded in the outer part of a pillar-like candle. The candle burns from within so that it highlights the natural designs put in the wax.

Are you excited yet? Candle making can be a fun and profitable endeavor and the designs you create are only limited by your imagination. Let's first take some time to learn about the history of candle making and then learn how make some cool candles, possibly to sell for profit.

Chapter 1: A Brief History of Candle Making

Candles have been used for utilitarian purposes and for religious ceremonies (and other types of celebrations) for more than five thousand years although the exact date that candles were first used is not known. They were used around 3000 BCE by the Ancient Egyptians. The ancient Egyptian candles had no wicks. These people used "rush lights", which were torches created by soaking the central portion of reeds in melted tallow or animal fat.

Eventually, the Egyptians invented wicked candles. The ancient Romans, too, developed wicked candles by rolling papyrus into a wick and dipping it in tallow or beeswax. As there was no electricity, candles lit homes by night and were used to help travelers find their way at night. They found their way into ancient Roman pagan religious ceremonies.

Even the early Chinese people found a way to make wicked candles by using rolled rice paper as a wick and molding candles in paper tubes. The wax came from a local insect combined with seeds. Several tombs of ancient Chinese rulers were found to contain preserved candles that were made from whale fat. They also used beeswax candles, dating back to about 40 BCE. Japanese also made candles out of a waxy substance extracted from tree nuts. In India, candle makers boiled cinnamon fruit to get wax out of it, from which they made candles.

The use of candles in religious ceremonies dates back many centuries. The Festival of Lights in Hanukkah has its origins in 165 BCE. Candles are mentioned in the Bible and, when Rome was Christianized in 300 AD, candles were used to celebrate Christian religious services like Easter Sunday.

While beeswax was in limited use before the Middle Ages, most candles prior to that time were made from tallow, which was rendered from cattle or sheep fat. By the Middle Ages, however, many candle makers strictly used beeswax, secreted by honeybees, to make their wax candles. Beeswax was preferred because the flame produced no smoke and there was no odor when the candles were burned. As beeswax was a limited commodity, only wealthy people could afford to use them; everyone else used tallow candles. They were also used in many religious ceremonies because they burned so cleanly.

In certain parts of the world where olives were plentiful (Southern Europe, the Middle East and Africa), people made lamp oil out of the olives and used a wick made of a substance that would burn and these were used like candles.

Candle making for the Europeans became a guild craft by the 1200s, particularly in France and England. Candle makers were called "chandlers". They traveled from one home to another, gathering fats from people's kitchens and combining the fat to make tallow for candles. Those who contributed fat received candles in return or were paid a small sum for their kitchen fat by the chandler.

In colonial America, colonists cleverly determined that by boiling the berries of the bayberry bush created a waxy substance that could be poured into candles and made clean-burning candles. The candles smelled sweet as opposed to the foul odor of tallow candles. This practice of making candles from the berries of the bayberry bush was soon abandoned because the process of making the candles was too tedious.

Whales and whaling played a big role in candle making in the 1700s. Fishermen who caught whales collected the spermaceti or wax created when sperm whale oil was crystallized. Candles made with spermaceti wax were clean burning but smelled terrible, like tallow. This was a wax that was hard enough to withstand the summer heat and burned longer than tallow candles. The very first "standard candles" which kept time were created from spermaceti wax.

Many advances in candles and candle making happened during the 1800s. About 1820, a French Chemist by the name of Michel Eugene Chevreul determined how to obtain stearic acid out of animal fat. This created a wax called stearin wax—a wax that was very hard and clean burning. Stearin wax candles are still popular today, especially in some areas of Europe.

A decade later, in 1834, Joseph Morgan invented the first device that could mass produce candles. Wax was injection-molded with a piston and then solidified. This allowed many candles to be produced at once and increased the affordability of candles for the common people.

In the 1850s, scientists found a way to separate a waxy substance from petroleum. The substance was refined and the end result was paraffin wax. It became instantly popular because it burned consistently and cleanly. It was cheap to make than any other type of wax, which made candles anyone could afford The major downside was the fact that paraffin alone had a low melting point so the candles didn't hold up well. This was when stearin wax was added to the paraffin to create a harder wax that burned clean and held up under the heat.

The 19th century was when wicks changed to become braided wicks. Prior to that time, wicks were made out of twisted pieces of cotton. They didn't burn well and they needed continual upkeep. Braided wicks burned so that the entire wick was consumed in the process of burning them.

The light bulb, powered by electricity, was invented in 1879. This meant that anyone who could afford electricity could afford to light their home with light bulbs and there were fewer candles produced until much later when candles were used for recreational purposes and became much more popular.

Candles made of paraffin and stearic acid were used in the first half of the 20th century. The oil industry became bigger and its by-product, paraffin was in wide supply. Mixed with stearic acid, the candles were popular as decoration and recreation. They were still used a great deal in religious ceremonies of all denominations. In the mid-1980s, candles came out with new scents and colors and they became popular as gifts for just about anyone. New waxes came out in the 1990s and this further increased the popularity of candles. For example, soybean wax was developed that burned more softly and slowly than paraffin wax candles. Palm wax was another new wax invented for candle makers. In fact, there is a wide variety of waxes—from vegetable wax to trendy gel waxes. Today they come in all sizes, colors, shapes, and fragrances for all to enjoy, mostly for pleasure.

Candles in History

People made their own candles for the most part until the Middle Ages when chandlers—professional candle makers—gathered animal fats from homes in villages to make tallow candles which were then for sale.

Candles were also used to measure the passage of time. They were first used around 850 CE by the Anglo-Saxon King Alfred the Great. These were "graduated candles" that were later called candle clocks. A candle was marked off and the king would divide up his daily time using the markings on the candle. Each "candle-hour" was marked by a ring around the candle and when the candle burned down a certain amount, the time was up and it was time to go on to something else. Eventually 24 hour candles were able to mark the time.

Timekeeping candles were also used in China around the year 1000 CE. Both sticks of incense and graduated candles kept a reasonably accurate time. In England, calibrated candles were used first around 850 CE. These types of clocks were also used as a type of timer. A nail was placed into the candle at the time the person wanted to mark the end of the time and when the candle burned down to the nail, the heavy nail fell, indicating the passage of a particular period of time.

One of the first major candle companies was the Tallow Chandlers Company in London, first established around 1300 CE. The company was eventually granted its coat of arms and got its first charter in 1484. It participated in making tallow candles that were used in lighting up the streets at night.

Chandlers or candle makers also sometimes went by the name "smeremongere". Smeremongeres also made vinegar, soap, sauces and cheese. Many also made beeswax candles to be used in churches and at royal events because they burned cleaner and without an odor. Candle making created a smell that, in some cities, making tallow candles was banned. In Paris in the 1400s, the first candle molds were created, which allowed for candles of different shapes.

Candle makers were able to make different types of candles by the 1700s to 1800s. Bayberry candles could be made which burned clean; however, it took 15 pounds of bayberries to make a single pound of wax. This made it impractical to do on a bulk basis. Whaling in the 1800s provided spermaceti wax for candle makers that allowed them to create candles that burned cleanly and bright. The first standard candles in the US were made using spermaceti wax.

Some candle makers used cheaper alternatives to spermaceti that came from rapeseed oil and Colza oil. These burned cleanly and were cheap to make. Stearin was then invented in 1811 by Michel Eugene Chevreul and Joseph-Louis Gay-Lussac in France. It was then patented and used to make candles.

A US patent was granted to Joseph Sampson in 1790 for an industrial device to mass-produce candles. He began to industrialize the candle making process using a cylinder that had a piston which injected candle wax and then allowed it to get hard before injecting more. He was able, with one device, to create 1500 candles per hour.

When paraffin was developed in 1830 (from petroleum products), it was eventually made into candles. The downside of these candles was their low melting point. By 1850, stearic acid was added to paraffin to make harder candles that stood up to the heat of the day and the heat of the burning wick.

As long ago as 1829, candles were made by Price's Candles, a company that made candles out of coconut oil and later, palm oil. The company was eventually bought out by the

Lever Brothers in 1919 and, three years later, a company called Candles Ltd was born. This company continued to make candles under the Candles Ltd label until 1991, when the candle making portion of the company was sold to another buyer.

Candles Today

With virtually no need for candles for lighting, candles are nearly as popular in today's homes as they were when candles were a necessity. Today, they are used for decoration, to create a romantic or personal ambiance, for birthday parties, other celebrations, and for religious ceremonies. Many decorative candles are scented so they make the room smell nice as well as look nice.

Today's candles can be made from a variety of substances including paraffin, soybean wax, palm wax and gel candles—all of which burn cleanly and safely for everyone to enjoy.

Chapter 2: Safety First

Candle Making Safety Tips

You can't begin making candles of any type (except possibly rolled candles) without first understanding a bit about candle making safety. As a hobby, candle making is generally quite safe. You just need to take heed of a few safety rules.

There are three areas of safety you'll need to consider: 1) using essential oils or other fragrances that can irritate your skin; 2) working with molten wax, which can cause fires and second degree burns; 3) spilling wax or other accidents. Basically, safety needs to be in the back of your mind at all times when making candles.

Cover your workplace with a tarp, an old cloth or newspapers. This keeps wax from dripping on surfaces that must later be scraped to get the wax droplets off. You need to keep your workspace as organized as possible so you know where everything is and don't spill anything unnecessarily. Have paper towels or newspapers ready to pick up major spills before they solidify.

Don't make candles without a fire extinguisher. You may need it for unforeseen fires. Make sure all your tools, molds, additives, accessories and ingredients are ready for use before you start the process.

Keep small children and pets out of your workroom. They might be at risk for tipping something over or getting burned. If you are starting to learn a new technique, have the directions handy and keep referring to them until you are skilled at the process. Mistakes happen most when you rush the process and either skip steps or make a careless error because you weren't focused on the task at hand.

Measure essential oils and other fragrances carefully and pour them without getting any on you. They are strong enough to stain furniture, irritate your skin or eat through plastic. It helps to measure them in advance, keep them out of the way and then pour them when needed. Use vessels for them that can't easily get knocked over. Wash your hands right away if they get exposed to these essential oils.

Similarly, be cautious in using colorants and dyes. While they are far less toxic than essential oils, they can make fierce stains on anything you spill them on. They are very concentrated; one to two drops are able to color more than a pound of wax so wear an apron and protect your clothes and other surfaces.

Wax must be treated carefully. The heated temperature of wax is approximately 180 degrees Fahrenheit, leaving you with serious burns if you get it on you. Wax doesn't boil as it heats up. It will just keep getting hotter until you begin to see smoke coming off of it. Use a double boiler so that your wax won't get too hot. Keep a thermometer handy to measure the temperature of the wax at all times.

Don't leave wax that is actively melting unattended. Wax can rapidly increase in temperature and you'll want to be close enough to it to turn the temperature down when needed. This means that you should never leave the room when wax is being heated up.

Candle Burning Safety Tips

- Don't leave a candle that is burning unattended for any period of time.

- Make sure children and pets have no access to the burning candle.

- Burn a candle on a heat and fire safe surface

- Don't burn candles near flammable surfaces, including artificial plants, lampshades or curtains.

- Keep the wick trimmed so it burns cleanly without causing smoke to waft up.

- Make certain the surface you're burning a candle in is a stable one.

- Keep debris like wick trimmings out of the pool of melted wax as these can burn.

- Keep the candle out of the draft or wind.

- Burn candles only the length of time that is equivalent to its diameter. For example, burn a 2 inch diameter candle only 2 hours at a time.

- When an inch or two is left at the bottom of a pillar candle or a half inch is left of a container candle or votive candle, throw the candle away. Do not burn them all the way down.

- If a candle is sputtering or the flame happens to be burning too high, it is a defective candle and you shouldn't burn it.

- Use a specially-made candle snuffer to blow out the candle. Do not actually "blow" out the candle or you can get embers flying through the air.

Chapter 3: Candle Making Supplies

In order to make candles, you'll need supplies for melting wax, wicks for burning, wax, fragrance, colorants and various items to shape your candle into a container or to create a taper. If you're going into the candle business, you'll probably want to have a variety of waxes and containers for molding the wax candles or creating a pillar. Let's start with the ingredients you'll need to melt wax.

Wax Melting Supplies

Make sure you have a fire extinguisher handy and that you have read the instructions on how to use it. Keep it in the room with you while you melt the wax. Remember what was said in the introduction: never leave melting wax unattended. Wax can start a fire at around 300 degrees or more so you shouldn't let your wax get above 250 degrees Fahrenheit.

You'll need a double boiler. This can be nothing more than a smaller aluminum pot inside a bigger one. The inner pot will contain the wax and the outer pot will contain a bit of water that boils at 212 degrees Fahrenheit so your wax can't get much above that point.

You'll need an accurate thermometer, much like a candy thermometer. It should tell you the temperature of your wax at various intervals. Don't let it rest on the bottom of the pan or the temperature will be inaccurate.

Wick Supplies

Without a wick to burn the flame, a candle is just a big piece of wax. Wicks can be made from paper, cotton, and hemp; the most common wick is braided tightly. Melted wax adheres easily to wicks and this is how tapered candles are made. Thicker wicks allow more melted wax to be drawn up around them so the flame is brighter. Wicks are measured according to their "ply" or number of individual threads. A 36 ply wick has 36 individual threads braided together and draws more wax up into it than say, a 30 ply wick. The flame will be larger with a 36 ply wick and will create a bigger pool of wax. A good wick will curl over to the side as it burns so that the candle smokes less.

A candle wick is the flammable pipeline that draws up the vapor from melted wax via capillary action. Once there is a pool of melted wax at the top of the candle, the melted wax is drawn up the wick and burns. Near the wick, wax vapors are breaking down, releasing hydrogen to make tiny unsaturated carbon chains that collect to form soot. It's the soot particles that actually burn. A good burning wick depends on the right amounts of oxygen and wax vapor near the wick.

You can buy spools that can create a wick of any size. The wick is cut off to the right length and affixed to an aluminum disc that sits in the bottom of the mold or container. You can also buy pre-made wicks that are precut to the right size and that are already affixed to the disc.

The highest quality wicks are plaited, knitted or braided so that the burn is slow and consistent. Twisted wicks are considered of lower quality than the braided or knitted ones.

Twisted wicks are loosely constructed so more fuel is wicked up into the wick. You'll find twisted wicks as part of birthday candles.

There are four different types of wicks:

- **Square wicks**. These are robust wicks that curl in the flame the way they are supposed to and are often used in beeswax candles because they block the clogging of the wick that can happen with certain fragrances or pigments. Square wicks are commonly used in pillar candles and in tapered candles.

- **Flat wicks**. These are plaited or braided wicks made from three bundles of wire. They self-trim by rolling over at the top as they burn and are the most common wicks you'll be buying.

- **Cored wicks**. These utilize a core in the middle of threads that are braided or knitted around the core. The wick is stiffer than other types of wicks. The most common core materials are paper, cotton, tin or zinc. They are commonly seen in pillar candles, jar candles, votive candles and devotional lights.

- **Special wicks or wicks for oil lamps.** These are specially made wicks that are designed to fit certain candle applications like insect-repelling candles and oil lamps.

In the US, about 80 percent of wicks are made entirely from cotton or are made from a cotton-paper combination. The rest have paper cores or metal cores with braided cotton around them. Wicks used to have lead cores until 2003, when they were banned from being sold in the US. Lead-cored wicks are still found in foreign candles. Now wicks that are cored are usually made of zinc or tin. They are mostly used in votive candles and container candles to keep the wick standing straight up as the wax solidifies.

Candle Wax Supplies

Of course you'll need to buy wax for your candles. Wax can come from just about any kind of fat, including oils, animal fats, insects, plat waxes and even rocks. A wax needs the following characteristics. In general, it must be a substance that is solid at room temperature but liquefies when the temperature is increased. It must be hydrocarbon-based and repel water. It must be completely insoluble in water. It must be low in toxicity and have no real odor of its own (or very little).

As mentioned in Chapter 1, candle "wax" was really tallow, made from animal fat. The only true "wax" candle years ago was made from beeswax. A type of candle wax was made as early as the twelfth century that was made from Coccos Pella—an insect. Spermaceti wax was created from the fat obtained from whales in the 18th and 19th centuries. By the late 20th century, synthetic waxes and gels were developed in order to make specialty candles. Also in common use were the vegetable waxes called palm wax and soy wax. These were made by hydrogenating (adding hydrogen atoms) to the oils obtained from the palm tree and soybeans. When you add hydrogen atoms to molecules of oil, their melting point goes down and they become solid at room temperature.

Paraffin wax is still the most common type of candle wax you can purchase and beeswax often comes in sheets to make rolled candles but is much more expensive than paraffin wax. Stearin candle wax can be obtained from European sources. You can also purchase soy wax, gels, palm wax, and synthetic waxes. There are blended waxes you can use for special purposes. All waxes available today are considered to be nontoxic.

Fragrance Supplies

Fragrances are made from many different things and can be natural essential oils or synthetic oil-based substances. Fragrance is commonly put into candles. In fact, 75-80 percent of all US-sold candles contain some sort of fragrance.

You smell the fragrance from a candle when the essential oil is evaporated from the pool of melted wax at the top of the candle as well as from the solid part of the candle. Other than releasing a fragrance, these types of candles burn exactly like regular candles.

Most oils used to scent candles come from a combination of synthetic oil fragrances and natural essential oils. If you choose to purchase fragrance for your candles, use only those fragrances that are specifically designed for use in candles. There are more than 2000 choices in candle fragrances available on the US market. All smell nice and are appropriate for use in candles. Some are also appropriate for use in soaps, perfumes, shampoos and lotions. They are basically nontoxic when burned in a candle but can be very harsh on the skin if you accidentally spill it on your skin.

If you want to make what's called an "aromatherapy candle", you need to use only essential oils of a specific type known to have a particular effect on the human body. You need also to use large enough quantities of the oil so that it can have an effect on the body or mind. Most candles that say they are "aromatherapy" candles contain synthetic oils and do not have enough essential oils in them to affect a bodily change.

If you use cheap oil, you might end up with one that burns more soot that an unscented candle. That's another reason why you should use quality fragrance oils that are specially made for use in candle making.

When you buy your fragrant oil, bear in mind that you can't just dump it in the wax without reading the directions as to how much to add to the candle. If you put in too much fragrance, the candle might not burn correctly. A good fragrant candle burns cleanly and safely with just the right amount of fragrance. Too much fragrance and you'll have a lot of soot coming off the candle.

You should know that all fragrance oils are tested for toxicology and dermatological safety. There is a Research Institute for Fragrance Materials (RIFM) that tests each fragrance material for safety purposes. It collects safety data on fragrances from all over the world and establishes worldwide standards for safety of fragrant materials. If possible, look for a fragrance that has been tested by the RIFM. Scented candles are completely safe when burning normally and give off only water vapor and carbon dioxide, both of which are completely non-toxic. The amount of fragrance given off is negligible when compared to the other two items.

Colorant Supplies

Most candles you'll find are not just white and instead are one or more of the many colors you can choose from. Candles can be white or ivory with the barest hint of coloration; they can also be in dark, deep jewel tones, metallics and multicolored hues. New colorants are being introduced every year to match changes in popular décor.

The color you choose needs to match the fragrance you've chosen and vice versa. People who buy your candles will expect that your cinnamon-scented candle will be red or bronze and that your "mountain breeze" candle will be a shade of pale blue or light green.

To complicate matters, the type and amount of colorant you add will vary depending on the wick you have chosen, the wax you have chosen and your fragrance. They make special pigments and dyes just for candles and you should use them in your candle recipes rather than dyes meant for another purpose.

There are dyes and pigments available for candle making. Dyes are different from pigments. Pigments coat the outside of a candle that is otherwise white inside. Dyes diffuse throughout the candle and the entire candle is the color of the dye.

Dyes come in liquid form and in powdered form. With dyes, you can create a light shade of a color or a dark shade of a color. Dyes burn easily so they won't clog up the wick with particulate material. In fact, dyes tend not to affect the way a candle burns at all so you can use them to get just the shade you want.

Pigments are actually microscopic colored pieces of material that are suspended in some kind of liquid. This is exactly like what paint is all about. They are painted on the outside of the candle to make the color you want to make. They don't fade like dyes do and they don't migrate or bleed once you apply the pigment. If you use a pigment like you'd use a dye, you will have a poorly burning candle that clogs the wick. Pigments are not meant to be burned. When you purchase a pigment, use one intended for use in candles and that are of a high quality, generally recognized as safe.

If the candle is otherwise correctly made, the addition of a colorant, whether it be a dye or a pigment, will not adversely affect the way the wick burns. Sooting, if any, is more a function of the length of the wick and the disturbance of the flame. Dyes can fade if exposed to the light, to different fragrances and to heat. This discoloration will not affect the way the candle burns.

Candle Molds and Containers

This aspect of candle making is when you can really get creative. Wax can be poured into just about any metallic or glass container. When it solidifies, it exactly fits the size of the container and is kept in the container as it burns. For this reason, it is not a good idea to use a container that is flammable. You can buy appropriate containers at a candle supply shop.

Molds are purchased at candle making supply shops. They come in many different shapes and sizes and are designed to be removed after the wax solidifies and before using it as a candle. They make aluminum, seamless candle molds that are short and squat, tall and thin or tall and thick, like you'd use for a pillar candle.

Votive candles need to be made in a mold. You can buy individual votive candle molds or molds that are lined up in racks for those who are making many votive candles for possible sale. Similarly, tiny tea-light molds can be made from aluminum, polyurethane or plastic.

You can purchase polycarbonate candle molds in globe-like shapes or other designer shapes to produce unique and special candles. Choose these types of molds out of polycarbonate because molds made out of this material hold up to the rigors of making multiple candles in them before they need to be replaced.

You can buy decorative cylindrical polyurethane molds that also stand up to the rigors of making many candles. There is a side slit that allows you to open up the mold and a hole at the bottom for putting a knotted wick through.

Taper molds can be purchased if you don't want to dip your own taper candles. They are made of clear plastic and have a hole in the bottom for the wick. When peeled out of the mold, they look as if they've been dipped.

Beeswax candle molds are molds for regular wax that create a textured effect that makes the candle look like a beeswax candle. They are split in half and hold together with rubber bands.

Molds for floating candles are made of aluminum, polyurethane or polycarbonate. Wax is poured into the fluted mold and the wick stands up as a cored wick. After it solidifies, the candle is flipped out and the mold can be reused.

Miscellaneous Items

You'll need a nice workspace that can afford to get messy or that can be covered with a tablecloth or newspapers. You'll also need dowels or pins that reach across the opening of the container or mold and allow the wick to stay in one place while the candle wax solidifies. You can get creative with ways to hold the wick upright and manufacturers of candle making products can supply you with the dowels or pins you need.

Have a notebook and pen or pencil handy to document everything you'll be doing in making candles. Candle making is a lot like cooking. You need to do test trials with varying amounts of ingredients. Write down the results in your notebook, taking special note of those trials that turned out the best.

You might wish to buy a digital scale to measure ingredients like colorants and fragrances. These are used in small amounts so a small digital scale would be perfect. Another purchase you might want to make is a hot glue gun for affixing pieces of wick to the bottom of a mold or container. Alternatively, you can buy "sticky wax" which can stick the aluminum disc holding the wick to the bottom of the mold or container.

The cost of materials necessary to start a candle business, including wax, colorant, fragrance, wicks, molds and the double boiler and other accessories can easily top a thousand dollars. That's a lot to put into a business when you aren't even sure that your product will be successfully sold to customers. If you're doing this as a hobby, you may not have to spend so much but the variety of candles you can make might be limited.

Chapter 4: The Basics

As mentioned in Chapter 3, make sure you begin by purchasing a journal and pen so you can document what you're doing. If you're going to do it right and make the same candle well each time, you'll want to experiment until you get it right and then write down a recipe from what you've done that will consistently make the candle that comes out the way you planned it.

What should you write down?

- The manufacturer and name of every wax, dye, fragrance, pigment, wick, wick holder, container or additive you purchase and use in the recipe.
- The amount of each product put into the recipe and in which step the item was put into the mix.
- The cooling time of the wax with all its ingredients in them.

- The presence of any imperfections like bubbles, cracks, flakes and white lines in the wax.
- The coloring of the candle. Is it what you expected and is it consistent within the entire candle?
- The fragrance of the candle. Is it too overpowering or too subtle and is it the fragrance you were expecting?
- After burning, note the burn time of the candle. Note the fragrance during burning to see if it is the fragrance you expected.
- Is the flame too big or too small? Is the flame smoking too much during burning?

Your first test should be of a small batch of candles because you really can't always expect the outcome and it may take several tests before you can make a larger batch of candles with a recipe you are happy with.

Beginning Candle Making

Clear away a heat source such as a stove or hot plate. Gather your materials, including paraffin (or other type of) wax, fragrance, colorant, wicks, candle molds a large spoon or dowel for stirring and a candy thermometer. It's very important to have a double boiler which can consist of a large pan with about 3 inches of water in it and a smaller pan in which you put the wax.

Ideally the smaller pan should have a spout or lip that allows the wax to pour in a small stream into the mold. The lip will direct the wax into the mold with great precision. Do not try to melt wax without a double boiler. With a double boiler, the highest temperature reached for your wax will be 212 degrees Fahrenheit or the boiling temperature of water. If you try to melt wax over a flame or a hot plate without using a double boiler, the wax will increase in temperature far above 212 degrees and, at about 390 degrees Fahrenheit, wax reaches its flash point and will boil, likely exploding all over.

One good device for melting wax is a Hamilton Beach Roaster. It has an inner pan that comes out and you can put water in the outer pan. It acts as a double boiler and can hold up to twenty pounds of wax at a time. Its cost is usually less than $50 and will last for many years. Smaller roasters can also be used as wax melters and are generally cheaper.

When melting wax, break it up into small chunks and put it into the smaller pan. Make sure that, as the larger pan boils water, new water is added to the larger pan so it doesn't boil dry. Continually watch the temperature and consistency of the wax. Use the candy thermometer to keep track of the wax temperature. Keep the wax away from the heat source so it doesn't burn or reach its flash point. Don't use the microwave to melt wax and, if wax is smoking at all, it is too hot and the vapors can ignite. Fragrances have a flash point as well so, if the wax is smoking, don't throw fragrance into it or you could have a fire.

Throwing in the Scent

How much scent do you need in your candles? Much of it depends on how strong you want the odor to be. A general rule is 3 percent fragrance per pound of wax or about a half ounce of scent by weight for every pound of wax. A half cup of scent in ten pounds of wax is another rule of thumb. This means you are using about 1-2 tbsp. of fragrance per pound of wax. All of this is added after the wax has already melted.

Fragrances have a shelf life of about 6-12 months, especially if kept in a cool and dark location when you're not using it. When adding fragrances, be wary of getting the fragrances in your eyes or on your skin. Some can be really caustic. Use fragrances in a well-ventilated place because they can be irritating to the lungs when breathed in. Some fragrances are brown in color and can affect the overall color of the candle, especially a lighter tinted candle.

Be sure and use essential oil or synthetic oil-based scents and not the block candle scents you'll see in hobby and craft stores. Such scents will make the candle itself have an odor but it won't throw off scent when you burn the candle, which makes it practically useless when it comes to having a scented candle.

When you're done making a test batch, you'll need to test the scent "throw" or how much scent the candle gives off when burning. For such a thing, you'll need to find someone to help you who haven't been making scented candles all day. Select a neighbor with a good nose and you'll be able to have them tell you whether or not the candle throws off a good scent.

Add both the scent and the colorant after the wax has been removed from the stove or roaster. If you leave the scent in the heat too long, the oil will burn off and you will lose the scent you put in. With colorant dyes, the heat can change the color you put in and you won't get the color of candle you had anticipated.

Remember that the thicker you make your wick, the greater is the pool of wax at the top of the candle and the more scent will be thrown off. Thicker wicks create aromatherapy candles if the right amount of essential oils is added to the wax. The longer it takes the wax to solidify, the less scent it will have. This is why you need to keep your wax temperature down—to 150 degrees Fahrenheit if possible. This shortens the length of time it takes the wax to solidify and will make the candle have the best possible scent.

Putting in the Colorant

Remember that there are dyes and pigments for candles. If you use dyes, you can purchase them in liquid form or in dyed blocks of wax that melt along with the rest of the wax and can be stirred into the candle to make the color uniform. Try not to use powdered dyes because they tend to settle at the bottom of the candle making the color non-uniform. Just drop in a few drops of dye and test the color you get. When you're happy with the color, write down how many drops you put in the wax, how much wax was used and be prepared for pouring.

Dye blocks are great for beginners. They contain a pre-made amount of dye in a small block of wax. Sometimes a color chart is included so you can add one block or four blocks, depending on the shade of the colorant you are adding. If you want to mix colors, put in blocks of different colors to create a new color combination.

If you're using pigments, remember that they are not soluble in wax but color the wax by means of dispersion. You need to buy pigment flakes and mix them in a wax that is about 185 degrees Fahrenheit. Your white candle is then dipped in the dispersed flakes, causing the outside of the candle you dipped to be colored. You'll need a container in which to melt the dipping wax that will fit the size of the candle you are going to dip. Experiment with how many flakes you need to achieve a certain color and, when you get it how you like it, write the recipe down.

Readying the Wicks, Containers and Molds

Ideally, you should be able to calculate how much wax makes how many candles but if you are making different sizes and shapes of candles, this may not be a worthwhile or accurate step. You need to prepare your containers and molds in advance because watching your wax melt and doing anything else is just not safe.

With containers, make sure they're clean and dry. Use a cored wick that is stuck to the bottom of the container by its aluminum connector piece with a piece of sticky wax. You can also use a hot glue gun to affix the cored wick to the bottom of the container.

Molds should also be clean and dry with excess wax from previous pouring scraped off. Some molds have holes in the bottom through which a wick is passed and tightly knotted at the underside of the mold. Cored wicks or regular wicks can be stuck to the bottom of the mold with sticky wax or a hot glue gun.

You may need to tie the top of the wick to a pencil or dowel so that it "defies gravity" and stays straight up in the mold. Wax tends to shrink as it cools so it's best to keep the wick affixed at both ends so it doesn't suck down inside the cooling wax.

Pouring the Wax

When you've removed the hot wax from the heat source and have added its colorant and/or scent, it is time to pour the wax. Carefully pour the hot wax into the containers or molds. Do it quickly yet carefully so you won't get burned. When you have finished, slightly agitate the container or mold with a hot pad so you won't get burned. This allows bubbles in the wax to rise to the surface and stay out of your candle. If you have a clear mold or container, gently tap the side of the mold where you see the bubbles and allow them to rise up.

Cooling Wax and Releasing Molds

If you're making a container candle, simply record the time it takes for the wax to cool and include that as part of your recipe. If you are making mold candles, you'll need to break the mold away from the candle. Because candle's shrink when cooled, you can fairly easily slip the candle out of the mold. Some molds have two halves that have to be separated before the candle itself is free. Try not to scratch or otherwise damage the candle as it must be perfect for it to go to sale. If your candle is pigmented, get your pigmented dipping wax ready and dip the candle into the dipping wax. Allow it to dry hung by the wick or standing on a newspaper surface.

Troubleshooting

There are a number of things that can go wrong when making candles. This is why you make test batches and do your best to catch mistakes as they happen. The following is a list of things that can go wrong in candle making and an idea of what you can do to keep it from happening again.

- **Mottling of the wax**. This is caused by too much oil in the wax. You should use a harder wax that has a higher melting point.

- **Air bubbles in wax**. This is caused by not tapping the bubbles out of the molten candle or having the wax cool too fast so the bubbles get trapped in the candle. Cool the candle more slowly by starting it out at a higher temperature at the time of pouring and you will have fewer bubbles. You can also tip the container or mold at the time of pouring to reduce air bubbles.

- **White frost marks on candle**. This means you used too much stearic acid additive in the candle. Make your next batch with less stearic acid and it will be better. It can also happen if the mold was too cold at the time of pouring or if you poured the wax beginning at too cold a temperature.

- **Candle won't release from mold**. This can happen if you didn't use mold release before pouring the mold or if you poured the wax at too hot a temperature. Use silicon spray or vegetable oil on the inside of the mold before pouring and check the maximum allowable temperature when using plastic or rubber molds. Don't re-pour over an already solidified candle and try freezing the candle in the mold because then it should pop out.

- **You have a sink hole in the middle of the candle**. This is sometimes a normal part of cooling a candle. If you warm the mold or container before pouring, there will be less shrinkage and, if you're careful, as the candle cools, you can poke holes in the top around the wick and refill the candle while it cools.

- **There are cracks in the candle**. This means the candle cooled too quickly. Cool the candle at a higher temperature, such as in a warm water bath. If you cool the candle in the refrigerator or freezer, this is when you'll get cracks.

- **Re-poured layers might not blend with first layer**. This happens when the second layer was poured after the first layer was too cool. Pour the second layer when the first layer hasn't fully hardened yet.

- **Pit marks or pock marks on candle.** This means that you put too much mold releasing oil or silicone on the mold. Wipe out the mold next time so there isn't so much material in it. You should also pour the mold at a lower temperature because hot wax can do the same thing.

- **The candle smokes when burning.** This happens when there are air pockets in the candle or when the wick is too big. Use a smaller size wick trimmed to one-fourth inch and pour at a higher pouring temperature.

- **The wick is drowning itself.** This happens when the wick is too small. Put in a bigger wick the next time.

- **The flame is too big or too small.** This is caused by a wick that is too big or too small. Change the size of the wick to achieve the flame size you're looking for.

- **Your melt pool can be too small or leaves leftover wax on the sides of the container.** This happens because the wax is too hard and has too high a melting point. Certain additives, such as hydrogenated vegetable oil, petrolatum, mineral oil or beeswax can lower the melting point. The wick can also be too small so think about a bigger wick.

- **The flame can flicker or sputter out**. This happens when water gets into the wax from the double boiler or the wick hole is not completely sealed at the bottom of the mold and water gets trapped in the wick area.

- **Oil Droplets can form on candle surface**. This can come from too much oil in the wax. Reduce the amount of oil you have in the wax and the problem should correct itself.

- **There can be insufficient fragrance when burning the candle**. This can be from using a fragrance that is too low in quality or quantity. You can accidentally burn off the fragrance by not putting it in just before pouring. Sometimes the fragrance cannot release into the air due to a higher melting point in the wax. Make sure the pool of wax is big enough to release fragrance.

- **The wax cannot adhere to the jar in places**. This means that you need to pre-heat the jars or put additives like beeswax, petrolatum or micro wax to the mix before melting it. Make certain that the jars are clean before adding wax. A heat gun can be used to heat the spots where the wax isn't adhering to even out the wax.

- **You can get a cauliflower knob on the top of the wick**. This is because the wick is too big for the size of the candle you are using. It will also cause the wick to smoke.

- **A crater forms in the center of the candle**. This is because the wick is too small for the candle or the wax burns at too high a temperature. Get a bigger wick and think about additives that make the wax have a lower melting temperature.

Now you know the basics of making the perfect candle. But making container candles or pillar candles all day isn't as exciting after a while. You'll want to experiment with more elaborate candles that challenge your new-found candle making skills. In the next chapter, you'll find "recipes" and instructions for building candles that will definitely be worth sharing.

Chapter 5: Making More Elaborate Candles

In this chapter, we will go beyond simple candle making and learn how to make candles that are more interesting and, therefore, more saleable if you plan on making the art of candle making into a business. Elaborate candles fall under the same chemical premises as ordinary candles. You get to use your knowledge of wick size, colorants, fragrances, and wax chemistry to create unique candles everyone will love.

Gel Candles

Gel candles were invented in the last thirty years and make unique additions to the candle making world. You purchase gel material in a tube or a bucket that can be squeezed out into a container with a wick firmly attached to the bottom of the container. What's unique about gel candles is the fact that the "wax" is translucent and you can put any number of flame resistant objects into the gel such as seashells, buttons and rocks. Gel can come without color or can already be colored with manufactured colorant appropriate for gel candles. If you are new to gel candle making, you can buy a kit that has the gel, wicks, color, scent and sometimes even the container.

Take a clear container and put a weighted wick in the bottom of it. Tie the wick to a pencil or small dowel so that it stands up appropriately in the container. Just squeeze the gel out of the tube it comes in and put in half of the total amount. Then place your "imbeds" or imbedded objects in the container and fill the container to near the top. You can use it immediately.

If you buy regular gel in a bucket, you'll need to make your candles the old-fashioned way. You'll need the candle gel wax, a weighted candle wick, a container, a candy thermometer and a heat plate or oven for melting the wax. Fragrance, colorants and imbeds also make for a great fancy candle.

Heat the gel to exactly 225 degrees Fahrenheit and use your thermometer. This substance melts much slower than paraffin wax so expect it to take up to an hour to get your gel to the appropriate temperature.

Prepare your clear glass container by cleaning it and adding a weighted wick. Gather your imbeds and have them handy. When the gel is at the right temperature add fragrance appropriate for use in gel candles. Use a half ounce of fragrance for each pound of gel you're melting. Add liquid dye or color blocks. Start with a little colorant and add more depending on how it looks. Dribble some colored gel onto a piece of newspaper to see if you like the color after it hardens.

Pour half the gel into the containers, add the imbeds and then fill the container to the proper level. Imbeds can be anything that isn't flammable, including molded paraffin items or paraffin cubes, seashells, glass figurines, art glass, marbles, cutouts of a different color of solidified gel, metallic objects, or glitter. You can put them at the bottom of the container or put them "floating" on a half-filled container. Imbeds open up the possibility of themed candles for holidays, special scenes and neat color combinations. Try not to put too many imbeds in the candle or it will look crowded. Enjoy these candles that burn longer than regular wax candles. Be aware of candle safety when making these candles because you won't be making them using a double boiler.

Soda Fountain Candles

This is a beautiful and whimsical candle that can be made with all of the ingredients you already have plus a soda glass like you'd see in an old fashioned soda fountain, a straw, a glass cherry or a paraffin-molded cherry. With soda fountain candles, you'll be working with whipped candle wax, the process of which will be discussed below.

Start with a clean soda fountain glass and put a straw in it. Make brown wax scented with root beer or cola and make the wax have bubbles in it by melting it at a lower temperature and allowing it to cool quickly. Then top it with whipped wax to look just like whipped cream.

You can also make a waxen fruit parfait by alternating layers of vanilla paraffin wax with layers of fruit-colored wax and you can include imbeds to make it look irregular. Top the parfait with a layer of whipped wax and you have a fruit parfait candle.

Whipped Wax

You can make whipped wax for the tops of sodas and parfaits or you can coat a plain spherical candle with whipped wax so it looks just like a snow ball. You can also make a mocha candle and top it with whipped cream wax. Ocean candles look great with whipped wax to look like sea spray.

You'll need the following items for whipped wax:

- Paraffin wax
- Corn starch
- A non-electric eggbeater
- A fork
- A double boiler
- A stainless steel bowl
- Candy thermometer
- Wooden stir sticks
- Fragrance and dye are optional

Melt the wax according to instructions using a double boiler setup. Use about one pound of wax as this is an easy amount to work with. When the wax has entirely liquefied, it is time to turn it into whipped wax. The paraffin should be exactly 160 degrees Fahrenheit in order to start the whipping process.

Add 1 tbsp. cornstarch for each pound of melted wax. If you are dyeing the wax, this is the time to do it. Add colorant slowly so that it gradually approaches the color you are looking for. You can't take the colorant out once it has been melted into the wax so go slowly. Add fragrance at this time as well. Use an ounce of fragrance per pound of wax.

Use the eggbeater to whip the wax to froth over several minutes. This aerates the wax and makes it look like whipped cream or whipped snow. You may do this step in the pot it was melted in or in a stainless steel bowl. It takes 5-10 minutes to beat the wax into the consistency of meringue.

If you are making a soda fountain candle, scoop a spoonful or two onto the soda-like wax. If you are making a snowball candle, take a solid spherical candle and, using a knife, spread the whipped white wax onto the candle until it is covered. It will look exactly like a snowball. If the wax solidifies before you are done, you can re-melt and re-whip the wax.

There are two types of sand candles. One type uses sand to shape a candle, but there is no sand on the completed candle. The other type of sand candle actually incorporates the sand into the finished candle as a shell.

Sand Candles

Sand candles are truly remarkable and fun to make. The candle will sit inside a sand shell created by super heating the wax and putting it in a sand mold. The supplies you'll need are as follows:

- Candle wax
- A bucket of sand
- Shaped items to use as forms in the sand
- Wick that is pre-tabbed or a wick that can be attached to a wick clip
- Double boiler
- Wooden stick for stirring wax
- Thermometer
- Optional fragrance and colorant
- One small spoon
- One large spoon or scooper

Use any shape you want to make a form for your sand candle. Start with wet sand and use a small bowl, candle holder or cookie cutter to create your form. Pack the sand tightly in the bucket or bowl and level it off. If the sand is too loose, the wax might seep through the sand and the sand shell will be irregular and too thick. Use the form to create a divot in the sand the exact shape of your form. It can be the shape and size of a small bowl or a candle holder.

If the sand isn't wet or compact enough, it will fall inward when you lift the form out of the sand. The thickness of the sand shell depends on how compact the sand is, how wet it is and the temperature of the wax during the first pour. You can wet the sand while the form is still in it to get a thinner sand shell.

You'll need to melt your wax using direct heat on the initial pour because you'll want a wax temperature of between 261 and 275 degrees Fahrenheit. Use your thermometer to get this perfect and avoid reaching the flash point of the wax. First melt it in a double boiler and then go to direct heat to get it past 200 degrees. At 200 degrees, take the melting pot out of the steamer pot and put it directly over the heat. Watch your thermometer continuously. When the wax reaches the above temperature (261-275 degrees), it's time to pour. A lower temperature sand at 261 degrees and wetter sand will give you a thin shell. A dryer sand

and higher temperature wax will give you a thick shell.

Don't add any fragrance or colorant to the first pour wax. The color will just be distorted by the excessive heat and fragrance can reach its flash point at those temperatures and can start a fire.

Use the back of the spoon so you don't splash molten wax into your mold. Fill the sand form up to the very top. Wax will seep into the sand forming the shell of the candle. Over time, the shell will solidify and then it is time to pour the rest of the candle in a second pour. The second pour involves using the double boiler and heating the wax to 200 degrees Fahrenheit. Add colorant and fragrance and pour the rest of the candle into the shell created by the first pour wax and sand.

There are additives you can put in the wax that create a solid and opaque finish. Additives can include putting a teaspoon of Vybar 103 or similar additive into the molten wax and then pouring the wax. One neat effect is to add Parol oil to the wax. This promotes mottling of the wax, which adds to the look of the wax. Put in 1 ounce of Parol oil into the wax and let it melt in.

The wax in your second pour should be between 190 and 200 degrees Fahrenheit and should have all additives, including fragrance and color well mixed in before pouring it. Deflect the wax with the back of a spoon in order to avoid splashing. After that, you place a tabbed wick into the melted wax and center it using a dowel or chopstick. Press it firmly into the warm wax and onto the sand shell it should sit firmly into or on the sand shell. You can tie the wick to a dowel or press it between two dowels or chopsticks to keep it stable. They make a wick bar that has a hole in it to place the wick. The bar stretches across the bucket and keeps the wick in one place.

You will get a sink hole as the wax cools. Re-melt the leftover wax and pour it into the sink hole to fill in the hole. Do this as often as necessary to make for a flat topped candle. Let the candle cool as much as possible between re-pouring attempts.

When the candle has cooled for several hours, it is time to remove the candle from the sand. Loosen the sand shell from the sand with a scoop or spoon. Don't scrap the candle. When the candle is freed, remove it by the wick and lift it to a newspaper-covered surface. Gently loosen free sand off the candle so you just have the sand shell and the candle left. Wash the candle off to remove free grains of sand and then let the candle dry.

Level the candle so it sits flat by placing a pie tin over a pot of boiling water. Put the candle on the pie plate until the bottom wax melts and flattens out the bottom of the candle. Swirl the candle on the pie plate in the position you want it to sit until it melts to the right level. Sand will come off the candle at the bottom but this is normal and will help level the candle. Finally, trim the wick to 1/4 inch.

Layered Candles

These can be fun and cheap if you save old wax from used candles and re-melt the wax to make the layers. Take a glass candle jar and put a tabbed wick in the bottom of it. Have the wick suspended from a dowel or use a cored wick, which stands up on its own.

Use your double boiler to melt one color of wax. Add extra color or fragrance if you want. Make the decision before doing the candle as to which layers will go in what order. Pour the wax into the container and let it nearly solidify. Wait about an hour before pouring the next layer. Repeat the above process for every layer until the candle wax reaches the top. You won't have much of a sink hole if the top layer is fairly narrow. Trim the wick to 1/4 inch and enjoy!

Ice Candles

Ice candles are beautiful candles made from a combination of colored waxes that look good together. You need to start with a paper milk carton that is trimmed to just above the height of the candle. Use a tapered candle as the wick in the center of the candle because there won't be any holes in it. Just drop it down inside the candle after it is poured or affix it to the bottom of the clean milk carton.

Melt the wax in chunks in a double boiler. Add dye chips when the wax has melted and then add fragrance when you are done melting the wax. You'll want enough wax to fill about half the entire candle. You can then pour out the water and tear away the milk carton if you want a single-color ice candle. If you want an interesting effect, pour out the water and melt wax of a different color. Pour the wax into one of the holes created by the ice cubes. The second pour will fill up the spaces where the ice cubes kept the wax away and the effect is beautiful.

When both wax pours have solidified, tear away the milk carton and trim the wick. Enjoy the beautiful nature of this interesting candle.

Balloon Candles

In this project, you will make a wax shell out of a water balloon and place small candles within the waxen shell or fill the shell with wax for a cool-looking candle. There are several things you'll need to gather:

- A small water balloon
- Wax that has a high melting point and that is basically translucent
- A pot to dip the balloon into
- Wire twisty tie
- Burner and melting pot; thermometer; stir stick
- Colorants and fragrances
- Protection for your eyes in case the balloon bursts and splatters wax on you
- Paraffin wax to pour into the higher temperature shell

Fill the water balloon to the right size with water. Dip the water balloon slowly into the molten wax at a temperature of around 250 degrees. The wax should go up to a point in the balloon that still has water in it. If you go above the water line, the balloon will likely burst. Remove the water balloon, let the shell dry and dip again and again until you have the thickness you are looking for.

Take the water balloon and shell; allow to dry. Then pop the water balloon and get the rubber and water out of the shell. Use the trick with the aluminum pie pan and boiling water described in the section on "sand candles" to flatten out the candle base. You can do this before or after filling the shell with melted paraffin wax. The end result is an oval-shaped candle that looks like a hurricane lamp.

Beeswax Candles

Beeswax candles are unique in that heat and melting are not involved in the candle making process. You end up with tall thin cylindrical candles, although you can also do a fatter, shorter cylinder.

You'll start with the following materials:

- Rectangular honeycomb sheets made from beeswax
- 1/0 square raw or waxed wick
- Scissors
- Craft knife
- Steamer pot
- Pie tin
- Hair dryer

Use a hairdryer to make sure the beeswax sheet is soft and bends easily. If it is cool, the sheet may break or crack during the rolling process. You can also pass it over a pot of boiling water to steam the sheet until it is pliable. Roll the candle in a warm room. Place a clean sheet of waxed paper underneath the rolling surface.

Place a wick at one end of the beeswax sheet. Tightly roll the sheet around the wick. Make the rolled over piece rounded so that it sets the stage for a round candle. Continue tightly rolling the candle so the candle becomes thicker and thicker. Heat up the wax with a hairdryer or steamer pot if it begins to cool.

When the beeswax sheet has rolled completely, press the edge of the sheet into the candle, effectively sealing the candle in a cylindrical shape. If the shape isn't perfect, warm the exterior of the candle and roll it into a cylindrical, smooth shape.

At the base of the candle, trim the wick flush to the bottom. At the top of the candle, trim the wick to 1/4 inch. You can prime the wick whether it is raw or waxed. You do this by cutting a strip off the beeswax sheet (the short side of the rectangle). Take this piece and melt it in a pie pan held over a steamer pot. Once the beeswax is melted, you can dip the wick into the wax, priming the wick for use in a burning candle. You can also flatten the base of the candle by placing the candle base on the pie pan to slightly melt and flatten the base.

Chapter 6: Candles as Gifts

You are only limited by your imagination when you choose to give candles as gifts. All of the candles described in Chapter 4 on elaborate candles would make great gifts. All they need is wrapping and a tag and you have yourself a great housewarming, Christmas or Mother's Day gift. Candles make presents that just about anyone can love and enjoy.

Let's look at a few more candles that make great gifts and then look at ways to package candles into beautiful gifts.

Lace-Trimmed Candles as Gifts

These look nice on taper candles or pillar candles that are cubic or cylindrical. You basically make an ordinary paraffin candle using all the directions we've discussed so far. Pastel colored candles look especially nice using this technique.

Purchase doilies of paper lace and cut one doily in half. Mold the doily around the base of the candle using double-sided tape to affix the lace to the candle. You can also affix the lace doily half to the mold and pour the wax with the doily in the mold. If the wax is translucent enough, you'll get a glimpse of the lace at the outer portion of the candle.

Easter Candle Holder Gift Idea

This is a candle holder you can make and use with a small pastel pillar candle. You can make the pillar candle in Easter colors using the directions already discussed in previous chapters.

For this project, you'll need:

- 1 inch plastic Easter eggs with holes drilled in the top and bottom and decorated with paints.
- 2 small round discs for the base and top of the candle stick holder.
- 3/16 inch dowel rod or slightly thicker
- Wood glue
- Drill

- Drill bits that fit the dowel rod diameter and another slightly larger for the eggs
- Pastel spray paint

Drill a 3/16 inch hole in the top of one wooden disc and in the bottom of the other wooden disc so that the 3/16 inch dowel will fit through the holes. Glue the dowel onto the middle of the bottom disc. Spray paint the dowel and the two discs completely.

Once the eggs have holes drilled out of them, string them onto the dowel until they almost reach the top. Use a saw so that the dowel is only so long as the eggs plus about 1/2 inch to insert into the bottom of the top disc. Glue the dowel into the top disc. When the glue has dried, you can top the candleholder with a festive Easter candle.

Make several different colored candleholders with different colored paint and different heights and set them together with candles on your Easter table. They also make great hostess gifts for the Easter hostess.

Christmas Gift Ideas

Two Christmas gift ideas will please anyone on your Christmas list. You can take the whipped wax ball described in the previous chapter and cover the ball in glitter so it looks like a shiny snowball. Use a clear, red or green cellophane square and put the snowball candle into the center of it. Bunch up the cellophane at the top of the snowball and tie it off with a ribbon of a contrasting color. Use a scissors to curl the ribbon.

Another great Christmas gift employs the use of a mold shaped like a Christmas tree. You use paraffin wax scented with evergreen and make several dark green evergreen candles. Then you whip together some paraffin according to the whipped wax recipe given in the previous chapter. Mix some glitter into the whipped wax or use glitter at the end of the process. Dollop bits of whipped white wax on the ends of the Christmas tree boughs to look like an outdoor Christmas tree. Wrap in cellophane as in the snowball example.

Baby Shower Candle Gifts

A great baby shower favor can be made out of wax. You don't even have to wrap them although you could wrap them in tissue paper with ribbon at the top just for fun. To make these fun candles you'll need:

As many cleaned-out baby food jars as you'll need for the party with the labels still on

- Paraffin wax
- Wicks
- Colorant
- Fragrance (banana would be nice)
- Double boiler

These will be container candles made in the fashion outlined in chapter 2. Add colorant to make the "baby food" candles, look like baby food and fragrance that fits for a baby food flavor. When the candles have cooled, cover them with their baby food colors and wrap if desired.

Gift Wrapping Ideas

Having the candle made is great but how do you wrap it so it's a surprise to those who receive your candle as a gift? As we described above, you can wrap the candle in cellophane wrap, bunching up the cellophane at the top of the candle, tying a ribbon to seal the gift. Curling the ribbon with a scissors makes a whimsical and colorful gift.

You can do the same thing with a couple of layers of tissue paper made for gift giving. If you have gift bags, you can put the tissue in the bags over the candle to hide its presence. You can also purchase acrylic boxes to house your candle masterpiece so that it can be stored when not in use. Wrap it like a regular gift to conceal the surprise.

Candles usually wrap easily and make nice gifts for anyone on your gift list. If you use molds, you can make candles of just about any shape or size and with all the colorants and fragrances available, the sky is the limit as to what you can do with candles you give away or sell to other people.

Chapter 7: Turning Your Candle Making into a Business

Let's say you've made dozens of candles in your kitchen or basement and now think you'd like to turn your candle making into a real business you can make money from. Candle making makes a great business. They sell well in gift shops and are a big hit during holiday seasons. But how do you start and what makes for a good candle making business? In this chapter, we'll look at how to start a candle making business and how to make it flourish.

Research the Business

You start any business with research. You need to give up your local craft store because you need to pay wholesale prices for the quantities of wax, colorant, fragrance and wicks you'll be purchasing and you'll want a wide variety of containers and molds to choose from. You'll also need to research the cost of bigger melting devices that can hold up to twenty pounds or more of wax at a time. Your Hamilton Beach Roaster might just do the trick or you may want to upgrade to a professional wax melting device.

Find a Supplier

Your candle supplier can easily be found on the internet. Use one that offers bulk items cheaply—as little as a dollar a pound, plus one that sells many molds, wicks, wick holders and other additives at amounts and prices you can afford. How much does it all cost? It depends on what you're planning. If you're making one or two types of candles, and you're not buying hundreds of pounds of wax, you can get by with a $100 or so to start your business. If you're making beeswax candles, the cost of the wax is higher so your start-up costs will be higher. You can also charge more for these candles than for paraffin candles.

Your molds are what will cost you the most when it comes to start-up costs. You might want to begin with a few molds and then add molds as you get more revenue. Ideally, your start-up costs should include a computer and possibly candle making software and business software so you can track your progress.

Look for candle making containers and molds at garage sales or flea markets. They're out there at a price you can't afford not to purchase. Containers especially can come from any type of container so keep your eyes open for bargains.

Don't Forget Your Time

Don't forget your investment in time when calculating your total profit. Your time is worth something, if not minimum wage. Candle making takes small chunks of time scattered throughout the day. You'll need time to melt the wax (carefully) and time to pour the molds or containers and then you can wait until it's time to re-pour any sink holes. Then, after another wait, you unmold you candles, trim the wicks, prime the wicks if necessary and package them for sale.

Plan for the days you'll be making your candles by having all ingredients purchased and your kitchen (or wherever you'll be making your candles) free of other obligations. That way you can make dozens of candles in one day and get them ready for purchase.

Create a Marketing Plan

Marketing candles is fairly easy because they are simple products that are found in many different types of stores. You'll have your best luck marketing your candles to small and locally-owned businesses that have similar gift items. Speak to the manager or owner of the establishment because they are the ones who have the buying power. If you've been a customer of this place before, all the better. Bring samples of your work.

Purchase business cards and include them along with candle burning instructions in every piece you make. Make sure the business manager and owner have your business card as well. Do everything you can to facilitate the selling of your product at their store.

What to Sell Your Product for?

You should be able to get between 100 and 300 percent profit on the materials and labor you put in, even if you sell them wholesale to a store. If you're new to the business, you need to determine the cost of your product. Write down the cost of your wax, additives, colorant and fragrance, and the cost of the wick. Your molds "cost" something in the beginning but as you use them over and over again, the cost per candle goes way down and is negligible over time. Include the cost of containers if you are making container candles as well as the cost of your packaging materials.

As a rule of thumb, it is a good idea to mark up the cost by 3-4 times your own costs for retail sale and twice times cost for wholesale items. In some locales, you can mark up your price higher than that such as really trendy stores or craft fairs. Include the time spent getting your supplies, making the candles, packaging the candles and shipping or delivering the candles.

Pricing can be a personal thing. If you overprice your candles, you won't get any buyers; if you underprice your candles, you won't get the profit you need and you will likely be devaluing your time. Be creative with packaging; make fun and unique candles with a good name or slogan to cap things off. People will pay more for something that is unique and different. Try to create a crafty and fun image for your company so people will respond to their value and quality and will find a reason to buy what you're selling over and over again.

Whom to Sell to

There are many options for selling candles and you can use any number of them. They include:

- Local gift shops
- Flower shops
- Craft shows and craft fairs
- Home candle parties like Tupperware parties
- Flea markets
- Fundraisers
- Open your own retail candle shop
- Sell off of a website by mail order
- Get contracts with larger companies to supply them with candles

Display your candles in a neat, yet creative way. Use other decorative items to enhance the way the display looks. Make sure that the candle display isn't too crowded and so that the customers can easily reach the candles when browsing for them. In your packaging of your candles, try to make sure that the scent of the candle is picked up by the customer. People buy candles by scent just as much as by looks. Have your business cards packaged in each candle and others stacked by the display.

If you're selling to a store, be friendly and shake the owner's or manager's hand. Tell them what a nice shop they have and let them see your free samples. Leave the free samples and a brochure with them and follow up with them in a week to see if they've tried the candles and if they're interested in purchasing any for their store. Try not to be pushy because that will only turn off a store owner. Make sure that when they buy your product that you have the volume of product they are looking for. You don't want to give them the idea that you're making these candles in your kitchen—which you might be.

Cater to the market area you are in. If "country" is in, sell country-themed candles. If "new age" is popular, make and sell candles that would be appropriate for a new age customer.

Keeping in Touch

Make sure you periodically stop by any stores in which you are selling your candles. You can make sure the display still looks nice and will give the owner an opportunity to buy new candles to fill in the ones they've already sold. If you have something new, bring them a new free sample and establish the perfect business rapport with your customer.

Conclusion

Candle making can be a great hobby that costs very little to begin. It is something you can do in your basement or kitchen and, if done correctly, makes a product you can enjoy at home, give to friends or sell to stores or flea markets. The sky is the limit when it comes to what you can do when making and selling candles.

Candles, as we've determined, have four basic components: wax, which can be paraffin-based, gel-based or beeswax; wicks, which are usually braided and sometimes cored; colorant, which can be a dye or a pigment; and fragrance, which can make a candle a wonderful thing to behold.

As you learned in Chapters 1 and 2, the value of wax and candle making safety cannot be emphasized enough. Wax does not boil but just increases in temperature as you heat it up. At some point near its flash point, it begins to smoke, sending off vapors that are highly flammable. When a wax reaches its flash point, it can spontaneously ignite or explode, leading to severe injuries and burns to anyone who happens to be standing nearby.

The fact that wax has a flash point is exactly why you never, unless you need to superheat your wax, heat wax in anything other than a double boiler. Water is in the bottom pan or in the bottom of a roaster and the top pan or layer contains the wax. Because water boils at 212 degrees Fahrenheit, your wax cannot be any hotter than that and you will be far from the flash point, which is approximately 390 degrees Fahrenheit for paraffin wax.

Candle designs are only limited by your imagination. In the chapter on elaborate candles, we talked about fancy candles like those made using water balloons and those that resemble snowballs and the froth on a soda in soda glass candles. Making whipped wax takes extra equipment and time but the effects on a candle are amazing. You can literally turn a boring spherical candle and turn it into a glittery snowball candle that makes a great Christmas gift.

If you want to make something truly different, buy sheets of beeswax, a wick and use something to warm the wax a bit. The entire project involves rolling the beeswax sheets tightly around the wick and pressing the end of the sheet into the rolled candle. The end result is something that looks like a tapered candle but was infinitely easy to make.

Candles also make great gifts. You can make gifts for people's birthdays or for holidays like Easter and Christmas using specialized molds and unique techniques. Candles are great stocking stuffers and are perfect to give away at baby showers and wedding or bridal showers. Just think creatively and the candle idea will come to you.

You may decide that candle making is a great hobby or something you can do to give away as gifts for friends or you may decide that candle making can be something more in your life. You may decide that you want to make candles in bulk and sell them wholesale or retail to stores, at craft fairs, bazaars or home parties.

In such cases, you'll need to establish yourself as a "Brand" and think of a whimsical title for your business. You'll want to have business cards made and think of creative ways to package candles that allow the customer to also be able to smell the terrific scents you've put into the candle. Remember that, with candles, smell can make the difference between making a sale and not making a sale.

You'll have to learn not only the art of making candles in bulk but you'll have to learn how to make a sale, whether it is to a business owner who will sell your product in a store or to a flea market customer looking for the perfect gift. The more fun you can make your candles and the better their presentation, the better your sales will be.

Take the time to determine the actual cost per ounce of making a candle so you can figure out how much each candle costs. Figure out how much time you're putting into candle making so you can "pay" yourself for being the candle maker. Don't forget the cost of delivering and wrapping your candles. Then set a price that is about 100 percent to 300 percent profit, pricing higher for those places that have high end items. You definitely want to get your money's worth out of making candles but make sure you are having fun, too!

Printed in Great Britain
by Amazon.co.uk, Ltd.,
Marston Gate.